TITANIC
GHOSTS OF THE ABYSS

"See the famous ship as real as life — for only a penny!"

Three-dimensional pictures were all the rage in 1912.

Many homes had 3-D viewers called stereoscopes.

Today, the *Titanic* still fascinates us — and we can still relive her story in amazing 3-D....

Hyperion Books for Children

A HYPERION / MADISON PRESS BOOK

The posters on the left:

THE LARGEST STEAMER IN THE WORLD

WHITE STAR LINE

NEW TRIPLE SCREW

S.S. "TITANIC"

WHITE STAR LINE.

"OLYMPIC." 45000 TONS.
AND
"TITANIC." 45000 TONS.
THE LARGEST STEAMERS IN THE WORLD.

To NEW YORK.
From SOUTHAMPTON, CHERBOURG, QUEENSTOWN.
To BOSTON.
From LIVERPOOL, QUEENSTOWN.

For Freight and Passage apply to
THOS. COOK & SON.
31, Fargate, SHEFFIELD;
16, Clumber Street and
97, Derby Road, NOTTINGHAM;
and Gallowtree Gate, LEICESTER.

The Titanic's STORY

She was the greatest liner of her time, a vast floating palace. The *Titanic* was larger and more luxurious than any other ship in the world — even her sister ship, the *Olympic*. The White Star Line had carefully planned every detail on the ship, from the dog kennels built for passengers' bulldogs and Pomeranians, to the squash court and steam bath.

Fifteen thousand workers had labored for two years to build her. When the hull (right) was launched, it was the largest man-made object ever moved. Once completed, the *Titanic* was 882½ feet long and as high as an eleven-story building, with space for 2,500 passengers. A ship this size was like a small city at sea, complete with its own hospital, barbershop, and post office.

(Above) Posters advertising the *Titanic*, pride of the White Star Line. The term "triple screw" refers to the three propellers that powered the ship through the water. (Right) The giant hull of the *Titanic* under construction in Belfast, Ireland.

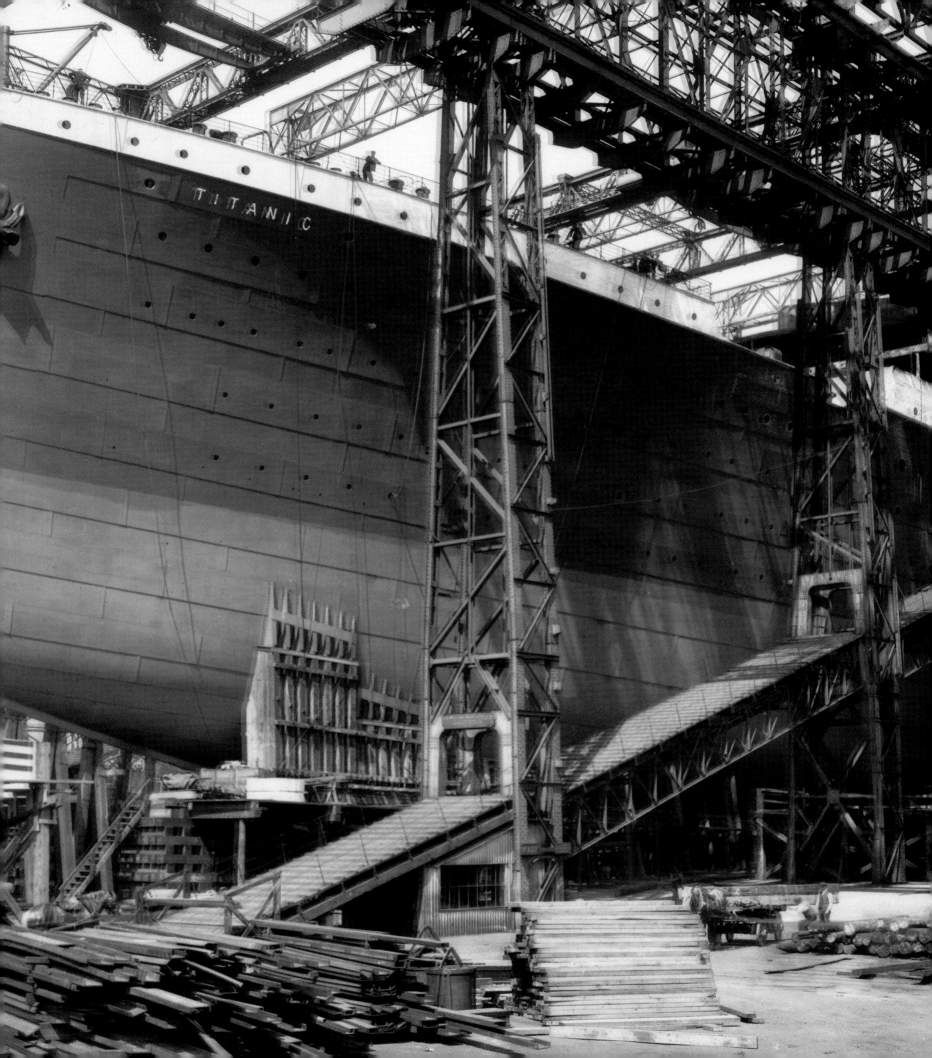

(Above) This baggage tag would have been placed on a piece of luggage a first-class passenger did not expect to use during the voyage. (Left) The *Titanic* looms above the pier on sailing day.

O n April 10, 1912, a special boat train brought passengers down from London to the docks at Southampton, England. Every class had its own gangway leading to a separate entrance into the ship. Boarding near the top of the liner were the passengers of first class, with their servants and mountains of luggage. Below them entered the second-class passengers, who were amazed to find that their rooms on the *Titanic* were even better than those of first class on other ships. Said twelve-year-old Ruth Becker, the daughter of American missionaries traveling home from India, "Everything was new. New! Our cabin was like a hotel room, it was so big."

Before the third-class passengers were allowed aboard, they were lined up and inspected for lice. Anyone found with the insects in their hair would be turned away at the docks. If they passed inspection, the third-class passengers picked up their own bags and boarded the ship through the lowest gangway of all.

On this first voyage, the *Titanic* carried 1,324 passengers and 892 crew. There were enough lifeboats on board for only 1,178 people. But everyone was perfectly confident that the *Titanic*'s sixteen specially designed watertight compartments would keep the liner afloat, no matter what.

In their free time, first-class passengers on the *Titanic* could sip hot broth on a deck chair, compose postcards in the Reading and Writing Room, or drop in for tea and cakes at the ship's French café. Those looking for exercise could visit the Gymnasium, which featured the latest equipment. Afterward, they could cool down in the pool (below), one of the first ever built on an ocean liner.

Exercise machines in the Gymnasium included an electric camel (right), stationary bicycles and a rowing machine (left, at right and center), as well as two mechanical horses, which stood in the corner.

On every landing of the Grand Staircase, passengers could admire elaborate decorations, like this electric candelabra (below). (Overleaf) The *Titanic* off the Irish coast on April 11, 1912.

"Grand" was just the word for the *Titanic*'s magnificent forward first-class staircase (opposite). During the day, sunlight poured through a glass dome overhead, glinting off the hand-carved oak paneling and elaborate gilt railings. At the top of the landing, a clock decorated with the figures of Honor and Glory crowning Time ticked away the hours. At 6 P.M., the ringing of a gong would bring the ladies and gentlemen of first class out of their rooms and onto the Grand Staircase. There they would pause for a moment, so that their elegant evening wear and jewelry could be admired by all, before gliding down the steps to dinner (above).

(Above) A copy of one of the many iceberg warning messages received in the *Titanic*'s wireless room. (Right) With the iceberg dead ahead, First Officer William Murdoch rushes to warn the men on the bridge (above left).

It was "a brilliant, starry night," said seventeen-year-old passenger Jack Thayer, describing the evening of April 14, 1912. The *Titanic* was steaming through calm waters at close to top speed, even though she had received warnings from other ships about the pack ice and large bergs that lay in her path.

At 11:39 P.M., a call came from the lookout, "Iceberg right ahead!" The *Titanic*'s wheel was turned sharply, but it was already too late to avoid a collision. The side of the iceberg scraped along the *Titanic*'s bow, opening its metal hull to the sea. If only the first four of the ship's watertight compartments had been damaged, she might have remained afloat. But the tear in the side of the ship allowed the ocean to rush into six of them. From here, the water could easily spill over into the rest of the ship. The *Titanic* was doomed.

Just after midnight, Captain Smith gave the order to load the lifeboats. But many people refused to leave, feeling safer aboard the giant liner than in one of the tiny boats. Later, as the ship sank lower in the water, some passengers began to panic and stampeded to board the remaining boats.

Many third-class passengers could not make their way up to the Boat Deck. Their path was blocked by locked gates. Some of them simply returned to their rooms to wait for the end (left).

Life jackets (below) were of little use to those who could not get to the lifeboats.

At about 2:18 A.M., the occupants of the lifeboats (above) heard a sound like thunder as the *Titanic*'s stern lurched high into the air and many objects inside the ship went crashing down toward the bow. At around the same time, the ocean smashed through the glass dome of the Grand Staircase (right), pouring into the heart of the ship. Amazingly, even this close to the end, the electric lights on the *Titanic* were still burning.

(Above) A brass White Star flag was attached to the sides of the wooden lifeboats.

As the *Titanic*'s bow was dragged deeper underwater (below, top), only the stern remained in view, pointing up at the stars (below, middle). Suddenly, there was a deafening crack, like an explosion, and the ship tore apart between its third and fourth funnels (right). The two pieces of the ship sank separately, spilling a trail of furniture, dishes, luggage, and chunks of torn metal as they made their way to the ocean floor (below, bottom). By the time the rescue ship *Carpathia* arrived at 4:00 A.M. to pick up the lifeboats, only 711 survivors remained from the more than 2,200 people on board.

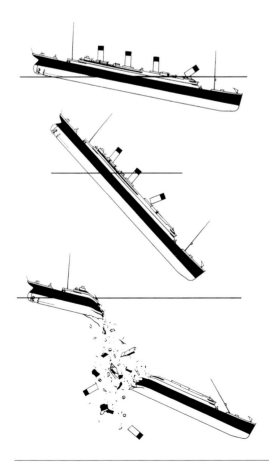

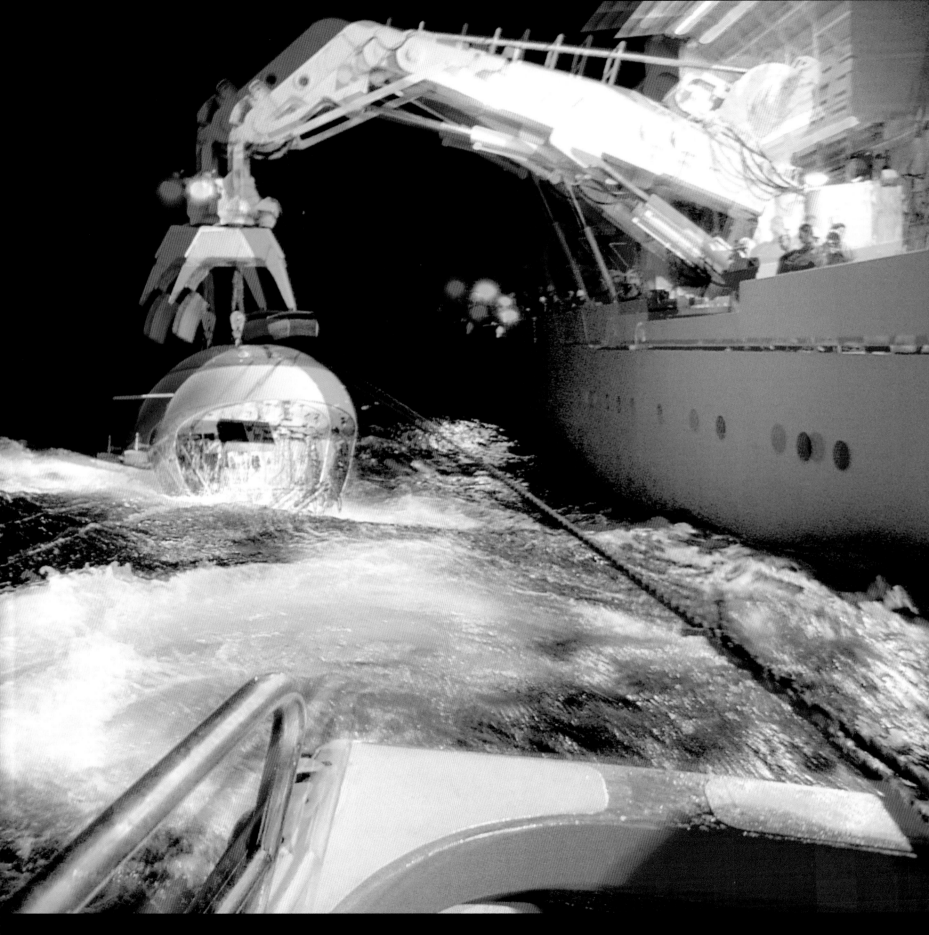

(Left) A crane mounted on the side of the Russian research ship *Akademik Keldysh* raises the submersible *MIR-1* from the Atlantic. (Top right) James Cameron, left, talks with Bill Paxton, narrator of GHOSTS OF THE ABYSS, after a dive. (Bottom right) Cameron climbs into *MIR-1*.

Return to the TITANIC

James Cameron had been to the *Titanic* before. While filming his 1997 blockbuster movie TITANIC, he had dived to the ocean floor in a small submarine to photograph the ship. But he was still haunted by the wreck. He wanted to see more. Would it be possible to look deeper inside the *Titanic*, to learn if any traces of the liner's splendor still remained?

Working with his brother Mike and a team of technicians, Cameron developed equipment specially designed to explore the *Titanic* in a whole new way. A giant overhead lighting system called "Medusa" would hover over the ocean floor. Digital 3-D cameras would record images for a large-screen movie that would make audiences feel like they were deep inside the *Titanic*. Best of all were the Remotely Operated Vehicles (ROVs) — two floating robots, or 'bots — that were small enough to explore parts of the ship where no other equipment could go. With the help of the 'bots (nicknamed Jake and Elwood), Cameron's expedition would be the first to see inside the *Titanic*'s exclusive parlor suites, staterooms, and public rooms.

O n his first dive to the ocean floor on *MIR-2*, Bill Paxton (above, at right) was amazed by the sight of the *Titanic*'s bow. He then watched as *MIR-1* moved in for a close-up of the *Titanic*'s prow (below).

(Right) A head-on view of the *Titanic*'s bow shows the prow and the rust-shrouded railings around the forecastle deck. For more than ninety years, undersea bacteria have eaten away at the metal structure of the ship, creating the "rusticles" that now cover much of her surface.

In the photograph above, workers stand beside the giant anchor chains that can still be seen on the *Titanic* today (right). The three largest anchors on the ship together weighed as much as twenty automobiles. The photo below, taken on board the *Titanic*'s sister ship *Olympic*, shows what this part of the ship would have looked like in 1912.

The *MIR-2* shines its lights on the capstans and windlasses used for securing ropes and chains on the *Titanic's* forecastle deck (right). The enormous links of the anchor chain are still in position.

The bridge of the *Titanic* was the control center of the ship. From here, Captain Edward J. Smith and his officers navigated the liner, guiding its speed and direction. Today, most of the structure is gone. All that is left is the bronze telemotor (left), which was once connected to the ship's main steering wheel. It was this telemotor that was cranked "hard a'starboard" on the night of April 14, 1912, as Quartermaster Robert Hichens made a desperate attempt to turn the ship away from the iceberg.

(Right) A crewman looks at the binnacle, which held a compass. The telemotor (left) was attached to the front of the binnacle.

(Top right) The 'bot Jake hovers near a rust-covered hole on the Boat Deck. (Right) The words "This door for use of crew only" are still visible on a brass sign on the Promenade Deck.

In the ghostly re-creation at left, Captain Smith (with beard) strides along the Boat Deck with his officers. The captain and members of his crew would have walked here daily, inspecting the ship, discussing her performance, and planning how far they expected to sail that day. By 1912, Captain Smith had been guiding liners safely across the Atlantic for twenty-five years. He planned to make the *Titanic*'s first voyage his last crossing before retiring.

Today, some of the davits used to lower the lifeboats still stand on the *Titanic*'s Boat Deck (below), ghostly reminders of the night they were last put to use (left). The Welin davits (right) were equipped to carry sixty-four lifeboats. But the White Star Line felt this would clutter the Boat Deck. So they carried only sixteen — enough for roughly half the people on board.

Once a lifeboat was loaded (left), the creaking davits would lower it sixty feet (eighteen meters) down the side of the ship to the ocean.

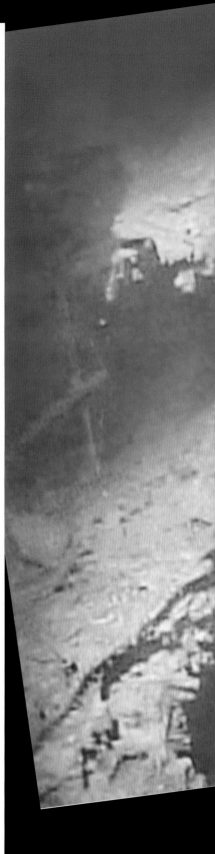

(Right) The Grand Staircase is now gone, leaving behind an empty shaft through which Jake and Elwood could enter and explore the lower decks of the ship. On the far right is the rusticle-covered wall where the magnificent decorated clock once stood.

Helped into their life jackets and directed by the crew, first-class passengers make their way up the Grand Staircase to the Boat Deck (above). By this time, some of them may already have noticed the seawater beginning to swirl up the staircase directly below them. Two-year-old Loraine Allison, seen being carried by her father at the top of the stairs, was the only child lost from first class. In third class, where many people could find no way to reach the Boat Deck, fifty three children perished.

This doorway (left) in the white-paneled Reception Room on D deck, was where many upper-class passengers first entered the *Titanic*. Here they could admire the custom-made carpets and leaded-glass windows before going up to their rooms.

Even after decades on the sea floor, the Reception Room retains touches of its former elegance. The elaborate metalwork on one of the door panels (above) is as graceful as ever. Traces of white paint can still be seen on the carved column (right) that still stands near the door.

On Saturday, April 13, 1912, first-class passenger Alice Lines chose to have coffee in the Reception Room after lunch. She overheard Captain Smith and J. Bruce Ismay, the chairman of the White Star Line, discussing what good time the new ship was making. At the end of the conversation, Ismay slammed his fist down on the arm of his chair. He told Smith that he thought the *Titanic* should be able to surprise everyone and get into New York a day early.

A phantom depiction (right) imagines this scene in the room today.

The Reception Room (top) was a pleasant place to sip tea among the potted palms and to listen to the ship's orchestra. (Bottom) Saucers for the Reception Room lie in a fallen cabinet. A cup and saucer (center) from another White Star Line ship show the identical china pattern.

(Left) Could this mirror once have reflected the image of a first-class passenger as she dressed for the last dinner ever served aboard the *Titanic*? A similar mirror is shown above in a color picture from a White Star brochure.

Every morning, the *Titanic*'s stewards brought to each first-class stateroom a fresh carafe of water and clean drinking glasses. They placed the glasses upside down to show they hadn't yet been used (right). Cameron and his team were amazed to see that the carafe and glass (above) had survived the sinking. The glass is right side up — meaning someone last drank from it on April 14, 1912.

Though most of Ismay's suite (left) has now vanished, the marble fireplace is still in good condition (right). A bronze bow (inset) decorating the top is still easy to recognize.

The *Titanic*'s four parlor suites were the most luxurious rooms on board. The suite that was occupied by J. Bruce Ismay (left), the chairman of the White Star Line, had two bedrooms, a sitting room with an electric fireplace (far left), and a private deck. Ismay stepped into one of the last lifeboats to leave the *Titanic*. In the days after the sinking, the newspapers nicknamed him J. "Brute" Ismay. He lived the rest of his life in disgrace for having survived when so many of his passengers died.

Deep in the belly of the ship, the *Titanic*'s stokers had the hot and filthy job of shoveling coal into the ship's huge boilers twenty-four hours a day (above). The steam produced by the boilers powered the liner's engines, as well as her electric lights. The work of these men and the ship's engineers helped keep the lights on the *Titanic* burning until just minutes before she sank.

(Right) These two views show the boilers as they appeared before they were installed on the ship (top), and as they look today (bottom). Some of the boilers fell out when the ship broke in two. These were photographed inside the wreck.

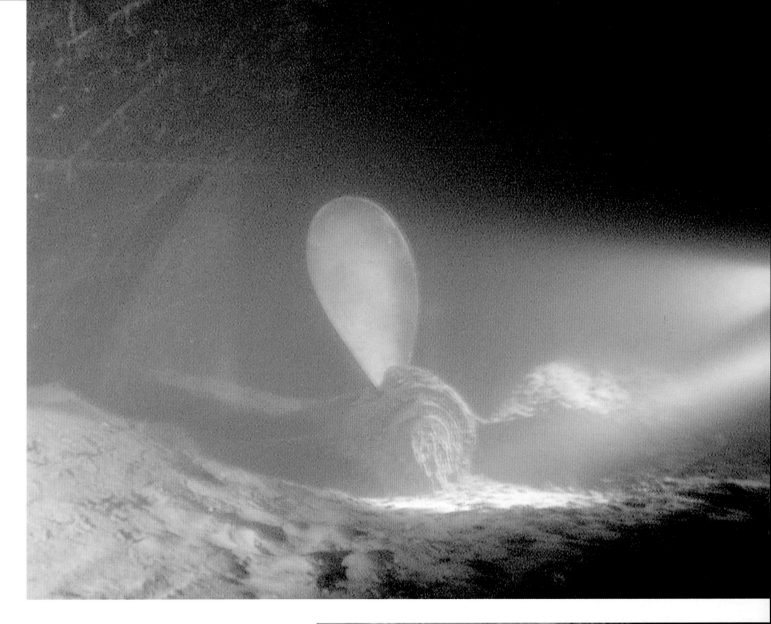

(Opposite) In February 1912, the nearly complete *Titanic* was floated into a dry dock in the shipyards in Belfast, Ireland. After the water was pumped out, workers were able to begin attaching three huge propellers to the ship's stern.

Lights from a MIR submarine revealed one of the *Titanic*'s three giant propellers, half-buried in the sea floor (above). Each of the side propellers weighed 38 tons and measured 23½ feet across. The center propeller was slightly smaller, weighing only 22 tons. Today, this propeller is completely buried in mud in front of the ship's rudder (right).

Before leaving the *Titanic* for the last time, James Cameron and his team placed a plaque on the stern (above) in memory of the many who died on that part of the ship. (Below) As the *Keldysh* sailed back to shore, Bill Paxton looked out over the wreck site and saw a white rainbow shimmering over the ocean like a ghost, a final reminder of the tragedy that had taken place there.

(Right) The recently completed *Titanic* leaves the Belfast shipyards for her sea trials in April, 1912. Though no one could have guessed it at the time, the "unsinkable" ship was soon to sail into history.

GLOSSARY

binnacle: A box or stand containing a ship's compass and a lamp.

bow: The front end of a ship.

forecastle: The forward upper deck of a ship.

funnel: A metal smokestack on a ship.

gangway: A ramp laid from ship to shore.

gilt: A thin layer of gold used to cover objects.

hull: The lower body of a ship.

prow: The front part of a ship, usually the tip of the bow.

rudder: A flat piece of wood or metal hinged vertically to the stern of a ship for steering.

rusticle: An icicle-shaped formation created by bacteria on the rusting iron of the *Titanic*.

stern: The rear part of a ship.

steward: A passenger's attendant on a ship.

submersible: A submarine that operates under water for short periods.

wireless: Another name for radio, often used in Great Britain.

PICTURE CREDITS

All color photographs are courtesy of Walden Media, LLC from *Ghosts of the Abyss* 3-D movie unless otherwise indicated. All paintings are by Ken Marschall unless otherwise stated.

KMC — Ken Marschall Collection
UFT — National Museums and Galleries of Northern Ireland, Ulster Folk & Transport Museum

Title page: (Bottom) Courtesy of Tom Deacon.
2: (Left and middle) KMC.(Right) UFT.
5: KMC.
6: UFT.
7: (Top) KMC. (Bottom) Brown Brothers.
8: Library of Congress.
12: (Inset) The Booth-Titanic Signals Archive, Wilts. UK.
15: Titanic Historical Society.
16: (Bottom) Titanic Historical Society.
18: (Left) Ken Marschall.
24: (Top) KMC. (Bottom) UFT.
31: (Top) *The Sphere*/KMC.
36: (Top) English Heritage, National Monuments Record. (Middle) KMC.
39: (Inset) KMC. (Bottom) Byron Collection, Museum of the City of New York.
40: KMC.
41: (Bottom) KMC.
43: (Top) UFT.
44: UFT.
47: UFT.

ACKNOWLEDGMENTS

Madison Press Books would like to thank James Cameron, Earthship Productions, and Walden Media. Special acknowledgments are due to Ed W. Marsh at Earthship Productions. Thanks also to Chuck Comisky, Len Barrit, Stephen Pavelski, Adrian DeGroot, Janace Tashjian, Claudia Huerta, and Justin Shaw of Earthship; to Al Lopez at Creative Logik; Ken Jones and Greg Oehler of CIS; Adam Howard of Complete Post; Roger Berger of Modern Video and Film; Debbie Kovacs at Walden Media; and to Ellen O'Brien, Don Lynch, and Tom Deacon.

Text, Design, and Compilation
© 2003 The Madison Press Limited
By permission of Walden Media, LLC
Paintings © 2003 Ken Marschall
Color photographs © 2003 by
Walden Media, LLC

First published in the United States by
Hyperion Books for Children
114 Fifth Avenue
New York, New York
10011-5690

First U.S. Edition, 2003

1 3 5 7 9 10 8 6 4 2

Library of Congress
Cataloging-in-Publication Data on file.

ISBN 0-7868-1899-9 (trade)

Visual and Historical Consultant:
Ken Marschall
Editorial Director: Hugh Brewster
Associate Editorial Director:
Wanda Nowakowska
Project Editors: Kate Calder,
Imoinda Romain
Art Director: Gordon Sibley
Graphic Designer: Jennifer Lum
Production Director: Susan Barrable
Production Manager: Donna Chong
Image Enhancement: Ken Marschall,
Ellen O'Brien, Colour Technologies
3-D Creation: Alter Ecom, Creative Logik
Universe, Earthship Productions
Computer Graphics: Creative Logik
Universe, Earthship Productions
Printing and Binding: Zanardi Editoriale

Titanic: Ghosts of the Abyss
was created in co-operation with
Walden Media, LLC, and
produced by Madison Press Books,
which is under the direction
of Albert E. Cummings.

Produced by
Madison Press Books
1000 Yonge Street, Suite 200
Toronto, Ontario, Canada
M4W 2K2

Printed in Italy